Colors in Christmas

A Fun Holiday Learning Picture Book for Toddlers and Preschoolers

Written & Illustrated By
Lil Rustle

Website: https://lilrustleworld.wixsite.com/lil-rustle

Special Bonus: As a fun addition, scan the QR code to visit our landing page to **download free coloring sheets** from our "Coloring with Shapes" Coloring Book! These sheets are a great way to extend the learning fun and improve motor skills.

This Colorful Book Belongs to:

____

Hello! I'm Leila!

Hello! I'm Finn!

Look around at all this snow –
let's build a snowman and watch it grow!

White **round** snowballs,

one **BIG**

one **small.**

Stack them up -

the head on top,

the body below.

One **orange** carrot,
shaped like a **triangle.**
Place it in the middle – here it goes.

Now our snowman has a nose!

Two **black** buttons **round** and small.
For the snowman's eyes,
let's place them all.

Now it can see us wherever we go!

Some branches for the arms,
two buttons made of stones...

and a red hat on top,
shaped like a triangular cone.

See how our snowman has grown!
HO! HO! HO!

It's getting chilly —
let's go inside before we catch a cold!

Look over there, what do you see?

It's **green** and **triangular,**
a CHRISTMAS TREE!

Let's decorate it, you and me!

One **yellow** ball,
bright and **round.**

Two **blue** balls,
sparkling and **round.**

Three **pink** balls,
pretty and **round.**

Hang them on the tree -
now it's your turn to count!

Add some glitter and a **golden star,**

our tree will shine bright from afar.

Next, place the gifts down below -
One **brown** **square** box, ready to go!

Two **purple** **square** boxes,

BIG and

small.

And three colorful boxes -
can you name them all?

Stack them neatly and look from the hall,

our tree and gifts are ready for all!

HO! HO! HO!
MERRY CHRISTMAS!
From us all!

Collect and Read them all!

COLORS IN SHAPES
SERIES

Fosters cognitive development,
nurtures creativity,
and promotes early literacy skills
in toddlers and preschoolers

Colors in Circles

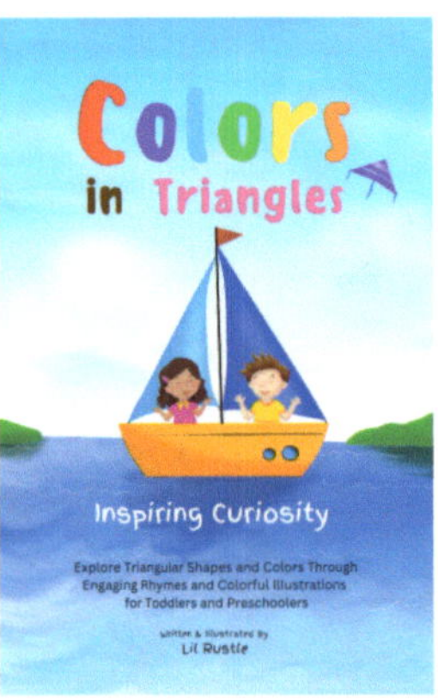

Colors in Triangles

Colors in Squares

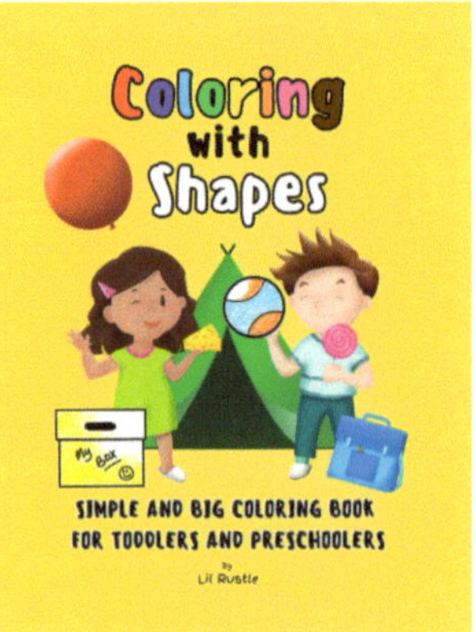

Coloring with Shapes

Colors in Circles

A Playful Exploration for Little Minds

Discovering round shapes with 10 vibrant colors in everyday objects for Kids Ages 1-5

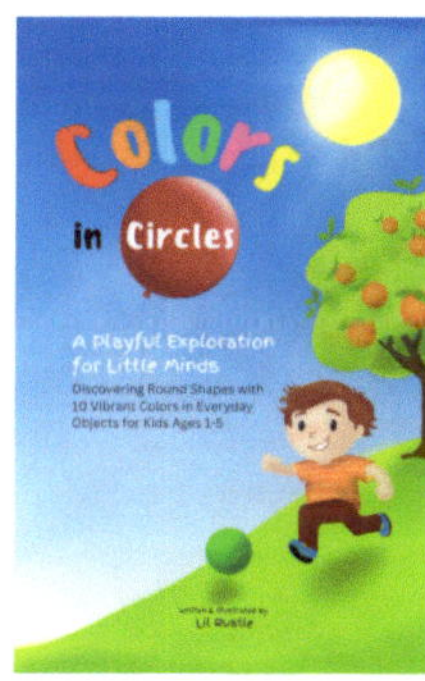

Beyond simply introducing concepts, "Colors in Circles" delights and encourages children to explore, ask questions, and foster a love of learning through engagement and curiosity.

Join our endearing protagonist as he curiously asks, 'What is (color) and round?' From the bright yellow sun to the irresistible pink lollipop, each page unveils vibrant colors found in everyday objects, nurturing early learning and language development.

Lil Rustle's approach goes beyond introducing colors and shapes by crafting a joyful reading experience. With rhythmic rhymes and repetition, the book aids in language development, while the lively illustrations make learning a visual delight.

Playful Exploration and Engagement

Discover 10 Colors and Everyday Object Connection

Rhythmic Rhyme, Repetitive Phrases and Vibrant Illustrations for Early Learning

Colors in Triangles

Inspiring Curiosity

Explore Triangular Shapes and Colors Through Engaging Rhymes and Colorful Illustrations for Toddlers and Preschoolers

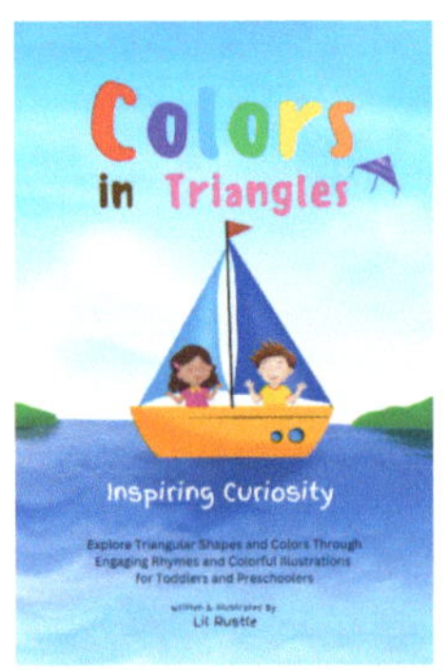

Beyond simply introducing concepts, "Colors in Triangles" delights and encourages children to explore, ask questions, and foster a love of learning through engagement and curiosity.

Join our endearing protagonists as they curiously ask, 'What can a (color) triangle be?' From the carefree purple kite to the irresistible brown chocolate, each page unveils vibrant colors found in everyday objects, nurturing early learning and language development.

Lil Rustle's approach goes beyond introducing colors and shapes by crafting a joyful reading experience. With rhythmic rhymes and repetition, the book aids in language development, while the lively illustrations make learning a visual delight.

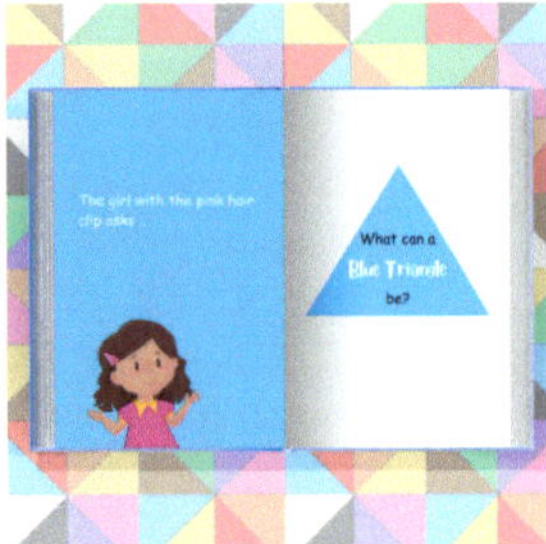

Playful Exploration and Engagement

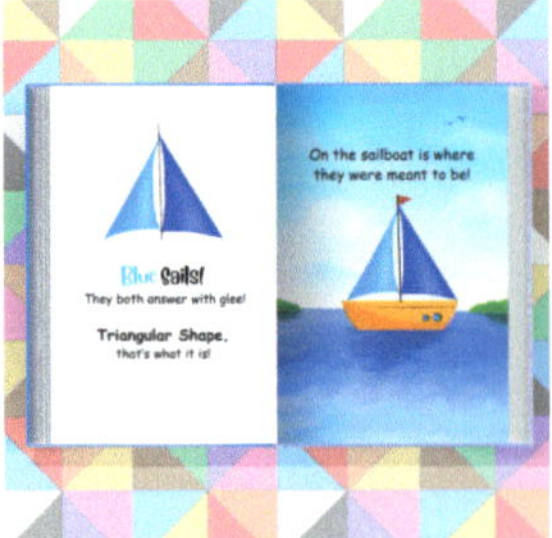

Discover 10 Colors and Everyday Object Connection

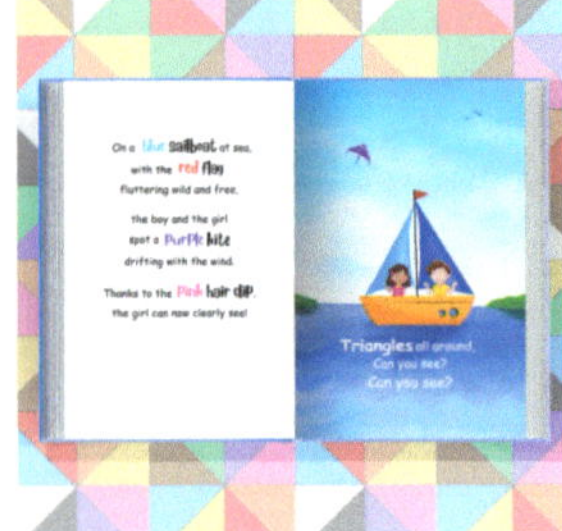

Rhythmic Rhyme, Repetitive Phrases and Vibrant Illustrations for Early Learning

Colors in Squares

Inspiring Curiosity

Explore Shapes and Colors with Playful Rhymes and Vibrant Illustrations for Toddlers and Preschoolers

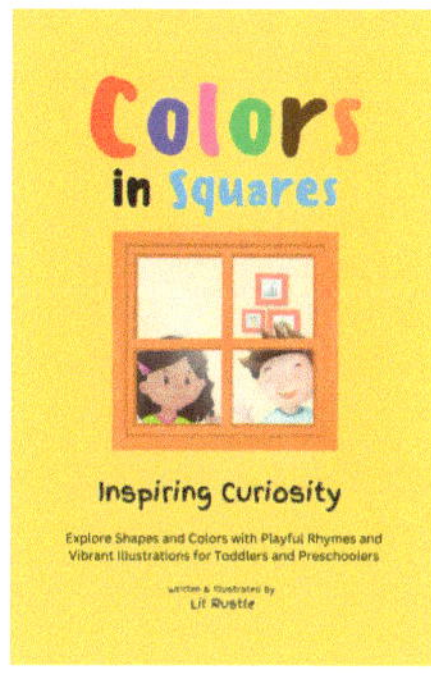

Looking for a fun way to teach your toddlers about colors and shapes?

Check out "Colors in Squares"—a lively book with bright illustrations and catchy rhymes!
This book does more than just show colors and shapes. It excites your child as they follow our cute characters asking, "What is (color) and square?" They'll see objects like an orange window frame and a yellow box, all while enjoying fun, rhythmic rhymes.

"Colors in Squares" makes learning enjoyable and helps with language skills.

Playful Exploration and Engagement

Discover 10 Colors and Everyday Object Connection

Rhythmic Rhyme, Repetitive Phrases and Vibrant Illustrations for Early Learning

About the Author

Meet Lil Rustle, a creative author and illustrator who loves crafting books that spark curiosity and joy. With a name that suggests lightness and playfulness, like the gentle rustling of leaves, Lil Rustle aims to create memorable experiences for young readers.

With an architecture background, Lil Rustle brings a fresh perspective to colors and shapes. "**Colors in Christmas**," a special edition from the Colors in Shapes series, showcases Lil Rustle's dedication to inspiring young minds through vibrant and educational content.

Excited for the future, Lil Rustle looks forward to sharing many more engaging books.

Your Reviews Matter

Dear Readers,

I hope you and your little ones enjoyed this book! Your feedback means a lot to me as I continue to create. Could you please leave a **review on Amazon**? Your review helps others discover the book and encourages me to keep crafting more engaging stories. Feel free to share your thoughts on social media as well! Thank you for being part of this exciting journey!

Warm regards,

Lil Rustle

Join the World of Lil Rustle

Be the first to hear about exclusive book reviews, new releases, special offers, and more. Sign up for my mailing list today to stay connected and never miss a thing!

https://lilrustleworld.wixsite.com/lil-rustle